Paramedics

IN OUR COMMUNITY

AMY ALLATSON

Knowsley Library Service

*Please return this book on or
before the date shown below*

Knowsley Council

You may return this book to any Knowsley library

For renewal please telephone:
Halewood 443 2086; Home Delivery Service 443 4202;
Huyton 443 3734/5; Kirkby 443 4290/89;
Prescot 443 5101; School Library Service 443 2679;
Stockbridge Village 443 2501

Like us on Facebook **https://www.facebook.com/knowsleylibraries/**
Follow us on Twitter **https://twitter.com/Knowsleylib**

Visit us on the web **www.yourlibrary.knowsley.gov.uk**
Join our online reading group **https://www.facebook.com/
groups/1152512218226037/?source_id=260694801821**

Contents

WORDS IN **BOLD** CAN BE FOUND IN THE GLOSSARY ON PAGE 24.

©2016
Book Life
King's Lynn
Norfolk PE30 4LS

ISBN: 978-1-78637-001-3

All rights reserved
Printed in Spain

Written by: Amy Allatson
Designed by: Drue Rintoul

A catalogue record for this book is available from the British Library.

What is a Community?

We all live together in a community. People in a community work together to help keep our local area clean and safe.

A TEACHER

There are many different people in a community, with many different jobs. For example, a teacher helps us to learn at school.

What is a Paramedic?

A paramedic is a trained person who helps save people's lives. They are part of the emergency services and work with police and firefighters to keep the community safe.

When there has been an accident, or a person in the community is very unwell, a paramedic would be called.

How do Paramedics Help Us?

Paramedics take people to hospital in an ambulance.

They can travel to any place where there has been an accident, or to someone who is unwell.

Some paramedics fly air ambulances. Air ambluances are flown to accidents they cannot reach with a normal ambulance.

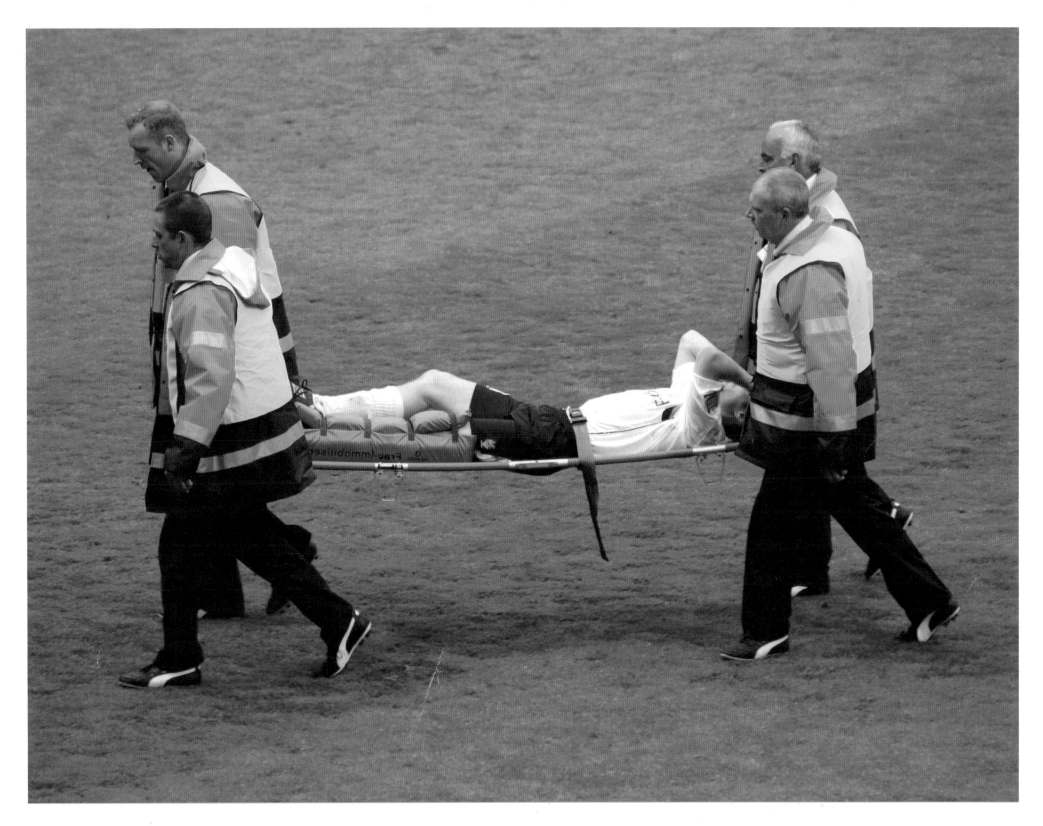

Paramedics work at events like football matches in case of an accident.

Where do They Work?

Paramedics drive and work inside ambulances.

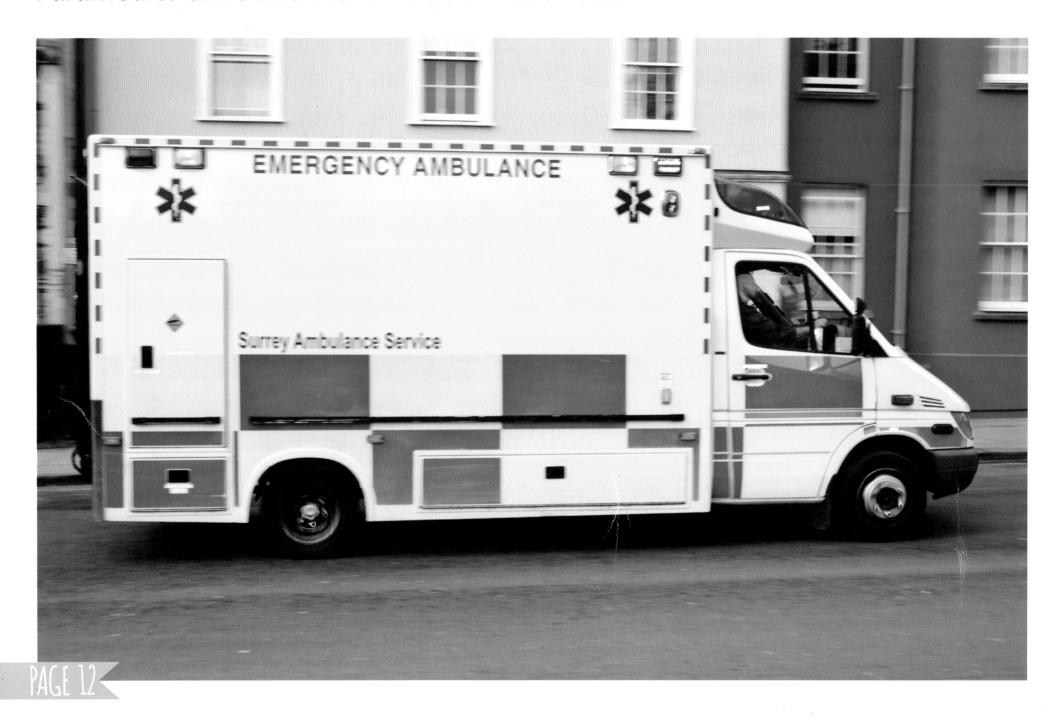

When paramedics are not using the ambulances, they park them at the hospital.

What do Paramedics Use?

Paramedics use many different pieces of equipment. They use stretchers to carry people to and from the ambulance

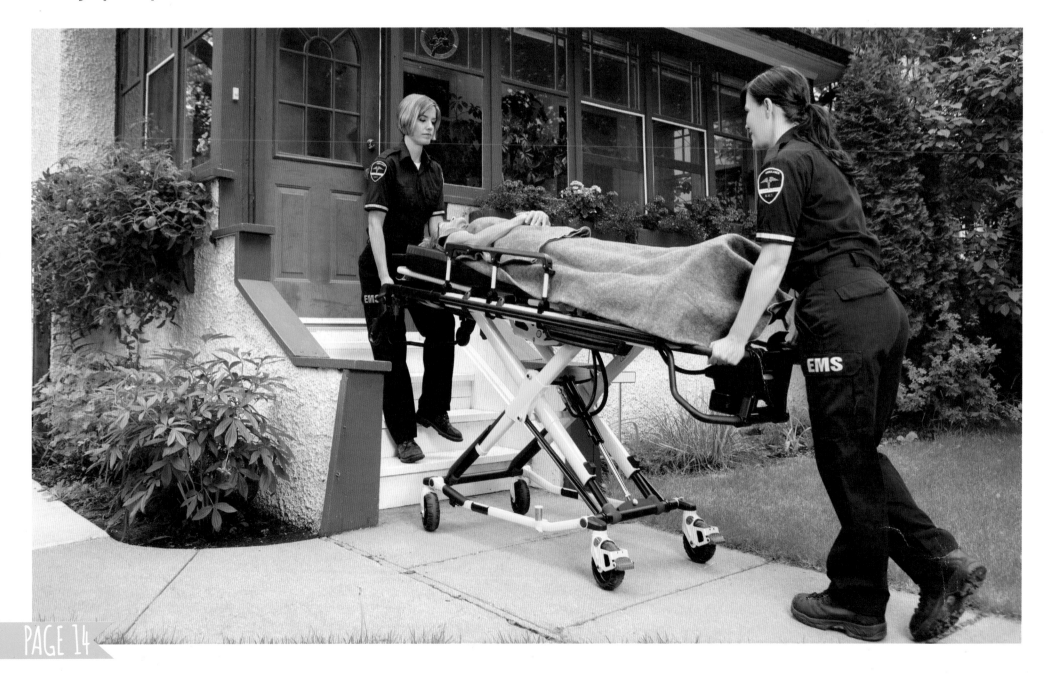

If a person is struggling to breath, paramedics will use an oxygen mask to help them feel better.

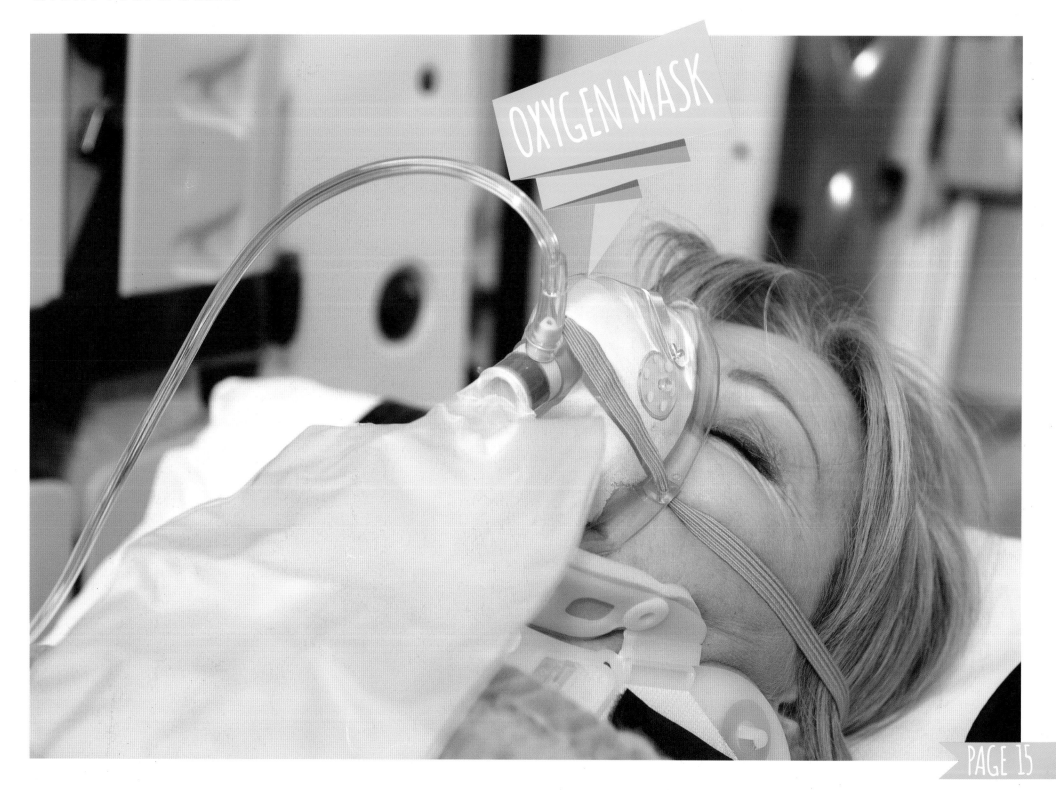

OXYGEN MASK

What do Paramedics Wear?

Paramedics wear a brightly coloured uniform.

Their bright uniform makes it easy to spot them at night time.

How do Paramedics Travel?

Paramedics travel in an ambulance. Ambulances travel very fast so they can get to people or accidents quickly.

Ambulances make a loud noise with a siren.

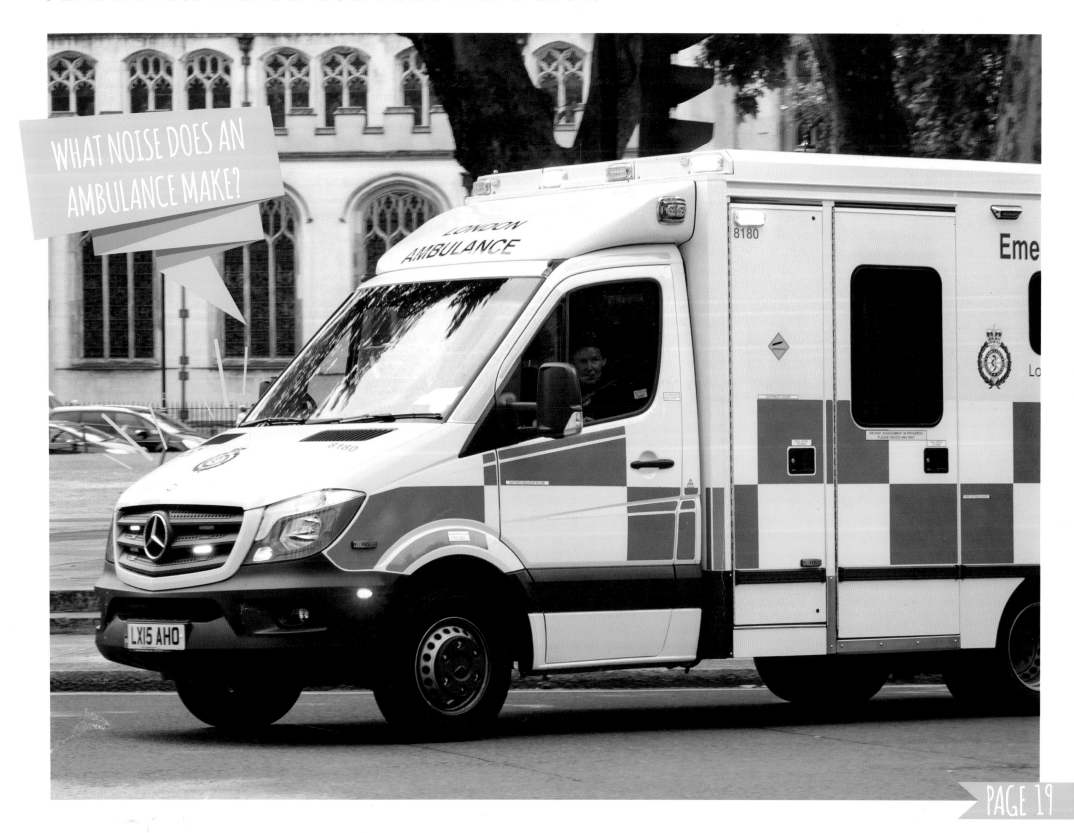

WHAT NOISE DOES AN AMBULANCE MAKE?

Inside an Ambulance

If you look inside an ambulance you will see a stretcher for carrying people and other equipment paramedics use for their job.

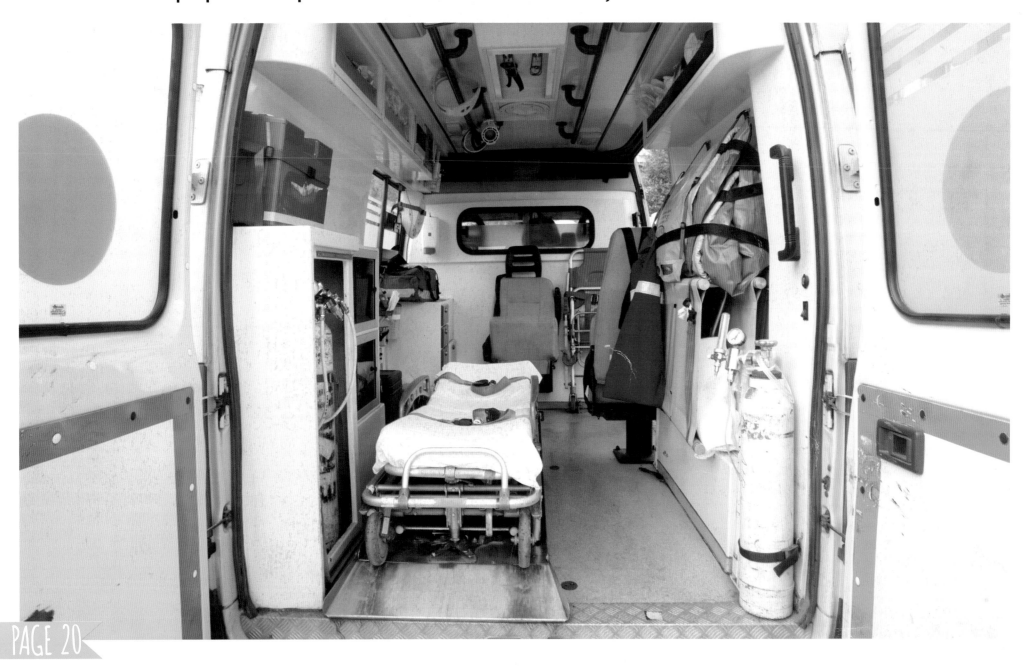

You will also see paramedics at work. They treat people while the ambulance is moving.

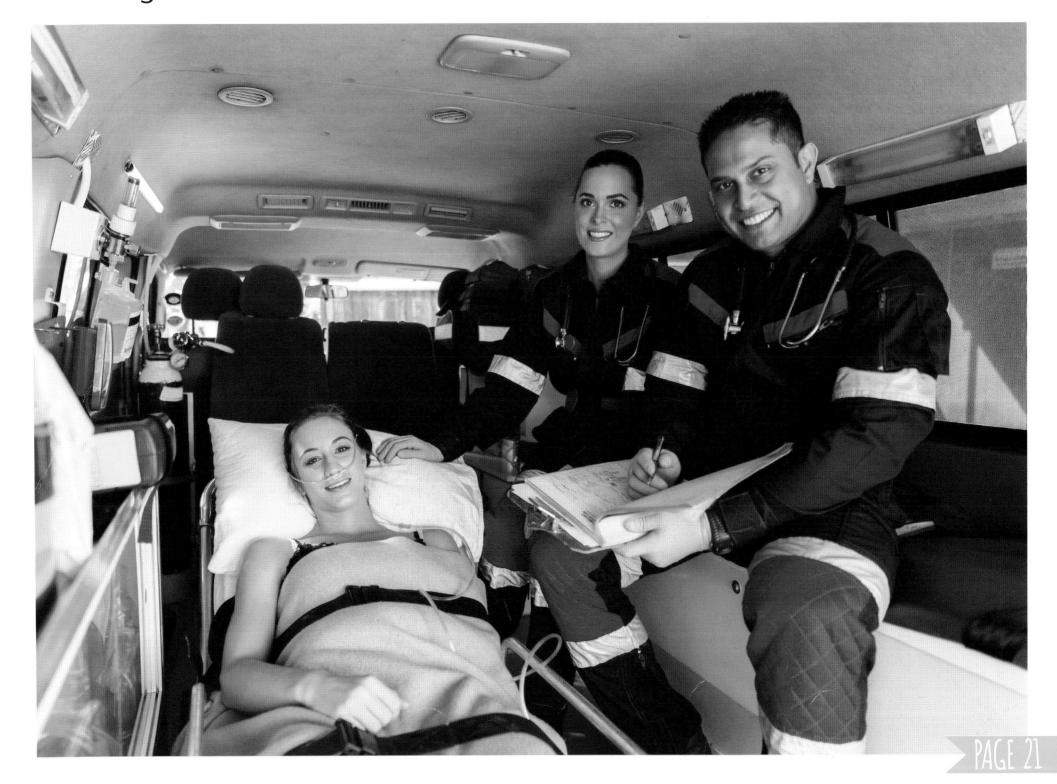

Can you Name...?

Can you name the equipment used by paramedics?
What do paramedics use them for?

Quick Quiz

1. What is a paramedic?

2. How do they help the community?

3. Where do paramedics work?

4. What do paramedics use a stretcher for?

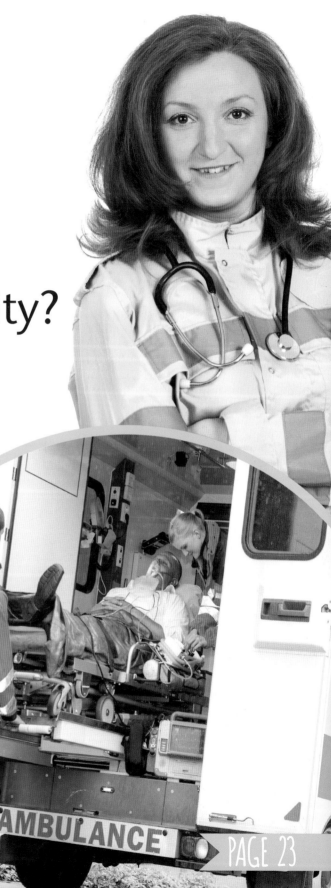

Index

Glossary

Community	A group of people who live in the same place.
Emergency services	People to call in an emergency, firefighters, police and paramedics.
Equipment	Things that people use to help them do their job.
Trained	When people are taught how to do a job.